WORLDfocus

Bangladesh
AMANDA BARKER

KU-252-062

Contents

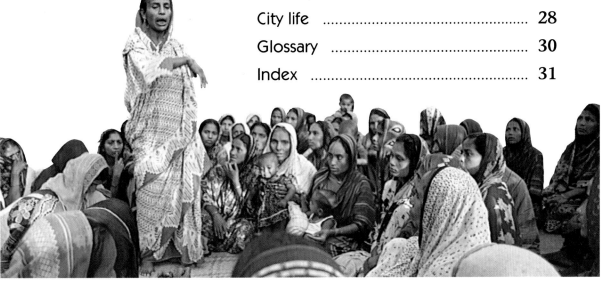

Introduction

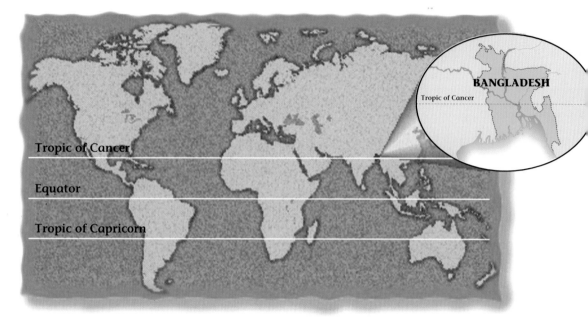

Tropic of Cancer

Equator

Tropic of Capricorn

BANGLADESH

Tropic of Cancer

Bangladesh is a small country in Southeast Asia. It covers an area of 144,000 square kilometres, which is just over half the size of the United Kingdom. Bangladesh is in the **delta** of the rivers Ganges and Brahmaputra (see map on page 3). Apart from a few hills in the north and southeast, the land is flat. In the south of the country there is a huge marshy forest called the Sundarbans. This forest is the home of the famous royal Bengal tiger.

Much of the land in Bangladesh is very fertile. Every year, after the heavy **monsoon** rains, the rivers flood and deposit rich soil along their banks. Most people in Bangladesh work on the land. They make a living mainly by growing rice.

Bangladesh has a population of about 110 million people. It is one of the most crowded places in the world. Only Hong Kong and Singapore have more people per square kilometre than Bangladesh.

The capital city of Bangladesh is Dhaka, where nearly five million people live. There are two other large cities, Chittagong and Khulna.

△ Where is Bangladesh?

▽ The River Ganges often floods. When it does, most of the land is covered water.

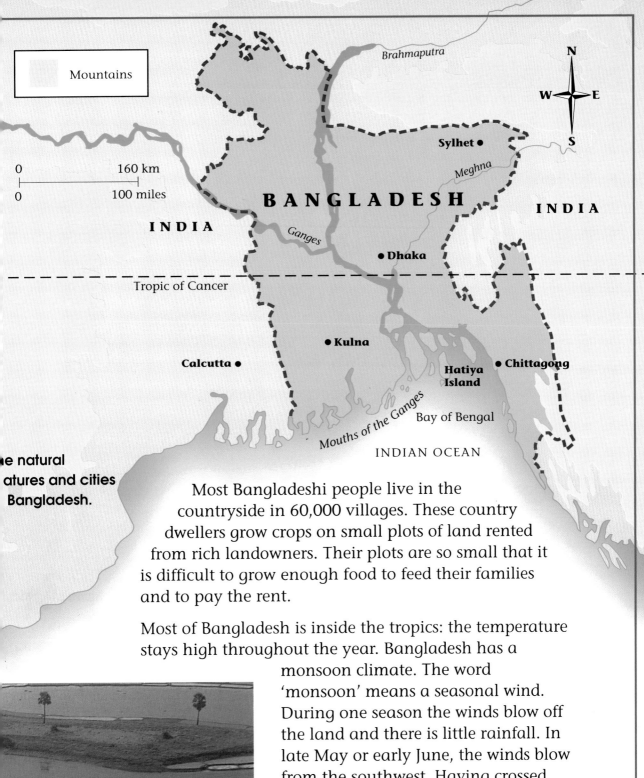

Mountains

0   160 km
0   100 miles

Brahmaputra

N
W⟷**E**
S

Sylhet •

Meghna

B A N G L A D E S H

I N D I A

I N D I A

Ganges

• Dhaka

- - - Tropic of Cancer - - -

• Kulna

Calcutta •

Hatiya
Island

• Chittagong

Mouths of the Ganges

Bay of Bengal

INDIAN OCEAN

...e natural
...atures and cities
...Bangladesh.

Most Bangladeshi people live in the
countryside in 60,000 villages. These country
dwellers grow crops on small plots of land rented
from rich landowners. Their plots are so small that it
is difficult to grow enough food to feed their families
and to pay the rent.

Most of Bangladesh is inside the tropics: the temperature
stays high throughout the year. Bangladesh has a
monsoon climate. The word
'monsoon' means a seasonal wind.
During one season the winds blow off
the land and there is little rainfall. In
late May or early June, the winds blow
from the southwest. Having crossed
the Indian Ocean they carry a lot of
rain and bring torrential downpours –
the monsoon rains.

Bangladesh has to survive flooding
almost every year from these rains.

The people

Bangladesh became a country in its own right in 1971. Until 1947 it was within the British Empire, and between 1947 and 1971 it was part of Pakistan. The word 'Bangladesh' means 'land of the Bengalis'. Most Bangladeshis speak **Bangla**. Most of the people have similar religious beliefs and follow the same customs.

There is a great difference between the rich and the poor in Bangladesh. Only a tiny percentage of the people are wealthy. Many of the wealthy are landowners who enjoy a comfortable lifestyle. Most of the population are poor. As they do not own land it is difficult for them to make enough money to improve their lives.

Religion is very important to Bangladeshi people. Most are Muslim, although about 14 per cent of the population follow the Hindu religion.

The Muslim religion affects the many farming families who own land. According to custom, when a man dies, his land must be split equally between his sons. Many farms in Bangladesh are very small today because they have been split again and again over the generations.

▽ **This poster in Dhaka is written in Bangla.**

△ A group of women perform in historical religious play.

Religion and tradition influence the lives of Bangladeshi women in many ways. After they are married they do not usually leave their village. They are expected not to work outside the home. Women do not usually do the family shopping.

Life can be hard for women who are poor in Bangladesh. To help themselves, many women have formed groups in the villages. Their aim is to improve everyone's standard of living. Development agencies, such as Oxfam, often give money or advice to these self-help schemes. Some groups concentrate on education. People are taught to read, or learn how to run small businesses, such as rearing chickens. Other groups may buy land so that rent does not have to be paid to landlords.

Where do people live?

Bangladesh is a small country. It is just over half the size of the UK. Bangladesh is also very crowded. There are twice as many people living in Bangladesh as in the UK, even though Bangladesh is much smaller.

The population of Bangladesh has been growing very quickly, while in the UK it has stayed about the same. People want many children in Bangladesh for a number of reasons. First, children are needed to help at home and to work in the fields. Second, one out of five babies is likely to die before its fifth birthday. People have more children to make sure that some will survive, and grow up to be adults. Lastly, children look after their parents when they grow old. This is important because there are no state pensions for the elderly to rely on.

Bangladesh has some of the richest farmland in the world, but this land may not be able to feed a growing population for many more years.

Most Bangladeshis live in the countryside. Only 16 per cent of Bangladeshi people live in towns and cities. The opposite is true in many richer countries like the UK. Most of the rural dwellers in Bangladesh live in villages. They have to rent fields in order to grow the food they need. Almost half the farmland is owned by a small number of rich landlords.

△ **People use the rivers for bathing and washing clothes.**

he people who live in the countryside grow rice and
ıte as their main crops. Jute is a type of reed which
eeds hot, wet conditions to grow well. People grow rice
) eat. They make household goods such as rope from
ıe jute, or sell it at the market.

Most of Bangladesh is flat farmland, and the population
; spread fairly evenly over the country. However, the
'hittagong hills in the southeast have slightly fewer
eople than average, while in and around the towns
ıere are more people than average.

ı Bangladesh there are only two cities with over one
ıillion people: Dhaka, the capital, has five million
eople and Chittagong has nearly two million people.
'ities will probably grow quickly over the next 20 years
.s people choose to leave the countryside to live in the
owns. They may feel pushed out of the countryside
ecause there is no land to rent. As a result, more and
ıore people move, or **migrate**, to the towns and cities.

△ **Many
people seek a
better life in the
busy towns and
cities.**

Agriculture

The soils in Bangladesh are deep and fertile. The temperatures are high enough to grow crops all year long. Most workers in Bangladesh work on the land. About two-thirds of all people working in agriculture either rent their **paddy fields** or are paid a small wage for 'day-labouring' on someone else's land. As well as rice and jute, sugar-cane and tea are also grown in some parts of the country. These crops may be sold and **exported** to countries such as the USA and Canada.

▽ Rice is grown in small fields. Most of the time these paddy fields are flooded with water.

Rice is the most important crop in Bangladesh. No land is wasted and the landscape is covered with small paddy fields. At first rice grows underwater, so the seeds are mostly planted at the start of the rainy season. The crops are carefully tended and usually harvested by hand.

Some of the richer farmers can afford to put in **irrigation systems**. Irrigation provides water for crops. Usually, a system of pipes or channels diverts water to the fields where it is needed. Farms with irrigation can grow up to three crops every year. They use new quick-growing rice seeds, and fertilizers.

But most farmers in Bangladesh are very poor. Only a few of them can afford expensive modern seeds, sprays and watering systems.

ientific advances in farming can
use environmental problems. Crop
rays may contain chemicals which
e harmful to humans and can
ak into the rivers. However,
ngladeshi farm workers could
crease food production with the
reful use of modern techniques. In
me villages, people have joined
gether to build a well or install a
mp. With the water, they have
en able to grow more rice.

any farmers also grow jute. Jute is
red in the river after the harvest.
ne bark rots and the stringy jute
res inside of the stalk can be easily
llected. The women in the villages
e jute to make household items
e hanging baskets or hammocks.
is also sold to earn money.

any Bangladeshi people live near
e sea or on the banks of rivers.
ney are able to fish as well as grow
ops. Shrimp fishing is important in
me coastal areas. Unfortunately,
ater pollution is an increasing
oblem. Waste is pumped into the rivers and this is
ashed into the sea. Fish catches are falling. Now
hermen often have to sail farther out to sea to fish in
eaner waters.

rming in Bangladesh could be improved, if land were
vned by lots of people, instead of just a few. There is
so a shortage of farm land. This makes every field
luable and expensive to buy. Some Bangladeshi farm
bourers have clubbed together to buy land, and some
ave been funded by overseas aid. This is a start, but it
only helping a few people.

△ Jute is kept
in water until the
stalks split open.

Industry

Bangladesh is far from being an industrial country. Very few workers are employed in factories full-time. However, as well as its rich farmland, Bangladesh also has good mineral resources which could be used for industry. For example, there are natural gas fields in the Sylhet area (see map on page 3). The gas is used for power in factories.

Jute, one of the main farming crops, is usually processed in Bangladesh before it is exported. Raw jute sold abroad would fetch a much lower price than jute which has already been made into rope or sacking.

There are 77 jute mills dotted around Bangladesh. These modern factories employ a few workers, but many more people work with jute in the villages. They make things like fishing nets and rope.

▽ Jute is being made into mat in this factory

Village women making hanging baskets from jute. This kind of work is known as a 'cottage industry'.

[ju]te used to be made [in]to sacks and a [b]acking for carpets, [b]ut plastic is now used [in]stead. As a result, [B]angladesh has not [b]een able to sell as [m]uch jute, and the [in]dustry has declined. As [p]eople become more [c]onscious of the [e]nvironment, they may use **biodegradable** jute again, [in]stead of plastic.

[In] Bangladesh paper-making is a [n]ew industry, and cement factories [h]ave been built. Bangladesh is also a [m]ajor exporter of manufactured clothes. [T]here is a steelworks and a shipyard on the [c]oast. Fertilizers for agriculture are being made from [n]atural gas, and Oxfam has helped to fund a drug [f]actory at Gonoshastya Kendra, to help provide [in]expensive medicines. However, most industries are not [p]roducing goods for export. Generally, the goods are [u]sed within Bangladesh itself.

The floods

Every year we read in newspapers about the flooding in Bangladesh. We also see pictures of the devastation on the television. Flooding disrupts people's lives in Bangladesh every single year.

The monsoon arrives in early summer. There are tropical rainstorms every day for four or five months. Sometimes the downpour lasts for days, sometimes for a couple of hours each day. Gale force winds, caused by a **cyclone**, whip the sea into a frenzy and cause tidal waves.

What is monsoon rain like? Imagine standing in a steamy place, under a warm shower. This is how it feels to be outside in the monsoon rain.

Most of the land in Bangladesh is flat delta land and is close to a river or near the sea. The rivers are full, even before the monsoon. In spring, the snow starts melting in the Himalayas. The meltwater swells the rivers as it is carried down to the sea. When the rains are heavy, the rivers often burst their banks. This floods the flat land. Tidal waves also travel up the rivers and make the flooding even worse. Many people cannot escape the areas that flood because there is nowhere for them to escape to.

In 1991 the cyclones were even more devastating than usual. About 200,000 people were drowned and around five million people living in the countryside lost their homes. Many survivors became ill with dysentery because their water supply had been **contaminated** by germs.

Emergency help reached Bangladesh quickly. During the floods the lives of many people were saved by relief food and medical supplies. The Bangladeshi government, other countries and charities like Oxfam provided the much-needed supplies fast. Lots of food was brought from parts of the country that were not flooded. However, the real work began as the land dried out. The people of Bangladesh had the task of rebuilding their villages, wells and roads.

In recent years, planning groups have formed in the villages. Together, the people plan for the rainy season. Planning is essential as there is no 'safe' land to escape to. For example, cyclone shelters have been built. These have been very useful in some coastal areas. After a flood, villagers join together to rebuild houses and mosques, and to repair roads.

Sometimes **development agencies** pay wages to workers to help with the rebuilding of villages. However, it is the Bangladeshi people themselves who do the work. They have shown that they can take control of their own lives by planning and preparing for the yearly floods.

◁ Nowhere is safe from flooding during the rainy season.

△ This family lost its home in the monsoon floods.

Hatiya Island

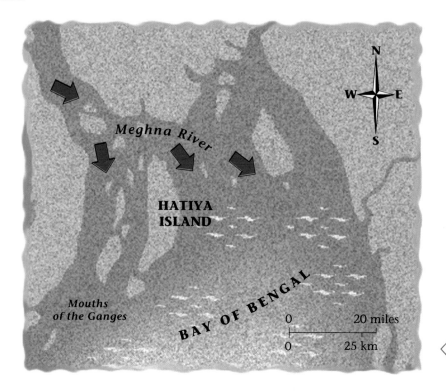

HATIYA
ISLAND

Meghna River

Mouths
of the Ganges

BAY OF BENGAL

N
W   E
S

0   20 miles
0   25 km

Hatiya Island
in the Bay of
Bengal.

Hatiya Island nestles in the Bay of Bengal, about two hours by boat from the mainland. It is 40 kilometres long and 13 kilometres wide.

Hatiya is a new island. Not long ago there was only sea where the island now lies. The rivers Meghna and Padma enter the sea nearby and the silt and mud they carry is dumped. Over the years this silt and mud make sand bars and islands like Hatiya all along the Bay. Hatiya is very flat and its land lies just above sea level.

The water from the Meghna river flows past Hatiya Island's north shore. When the river is full, the land on this coast is eaten away by the river. At the same time mud and sand carried by the river is dumped on Hatiya Island's south shore. As land is removed in the north and built up in the south, the whole island is shifting southwards.

About 300,000 people live on Hatiya Island. Many of these people have to rent land to grow the rice they need for their families.

△ There are many villages like this on Hatiya Island.

There is only one road running through the island. It runs from the north to the south. It is muddy and impossible to use during the rainy season. There is no hospital on the island. It was washed away by floods in 1981.

△ Homes are built on raised banks to protect them against the floods.

Hatiya Island has faced more than its fair share of problems. It lies right in the path of the cyclones. Tidal waves have swept across the flat land many times. In April 1991 a tidal wave overturned buses and destroyed bridges, and washed many people out to sea. Everyone living on the island has a tale of suffering to tell.

Hatiya Island's main strength is its people. They have rebuilt their homes and lives many times.

Some villages have been built on **killah** land (land that has been raised to protect it from flooding). The water channel is only a few metres from people's doorsteps.

Some villages have a cyclone shelter. A village may have about 200 homes, a mosque and a tea-shop.

Village life

On Hatiya Island, as in the whole of Bangladesh, women lead very different lives to the men. The women traditionally stay in the home while men do all the jobs which involve leaving the house, such as the shopping. Some development agencies are concentrating on improving the lives of women, and women's groups have become very important over the last few years. Some groups have jointly bought 'new' land that is formed from mud and silt deposited by rivers.

A woman's work starts early in the morning. Before the children get up, she feeds her chickens. She has had to save up to buy them. But she now makes a profit selling the eggs in the village market-place. Five years ago a woman would never have done this. Women have also started farming land themselves. They have proved to the men that they can grow a good crop of rice, too.

Most of the women in the village work very hard during the day. To make money they weave hanging baskets or make mats from jute, and take the outer husks off rice. Most families are large and a new baby may be born every other year. It can be hard work for a mother to look after the younger children, although women in the village will take it in turns to help each other out.

Sabjada Kho who lives in Batenkhali o Hatiya Islan breeds chickens and sells their eg to make money her family.

△ **The catch is poor for these fishermen. Pollution might be the cause.**

though some women work on the land, it is mainly
en and boys who do this kind of work. Rice and jute
e the main crops, but people grow fruit, lentils and
etel nuts too. Many of the men travel to the coast to
h. In recent years they have caught fewer fish in their
ets. This drop in the number of fish has been blamed
n the growing amount of pollution in the Bay of
engal. Rivers carry sewage and factory waste to the sea.
his pollution can kill fish.

he tea-shop is the most important meeting place in the
llage. People go there to listen to the news on the radio
nd to talk. The mosque is visited daily by the men. The
nam, or Muslim priest, is probably the most important
erson in the village.

'ery village has a cyclone warden. This is only a part-
ne job, but it is the warden's duty to warn villagers of
storm. There is also a midwife in every village, as no
ie goes to a hospital to have their baby.

School

Not everyone gets the chance of a good education in Bangladesh. Being able to read, write and to do simple sums helps people make a better life for themselves and their families. But in Bangladesh only half of the men and a quarter of the women can read and write. About 60 per cent of all children start primary school, but most of these are boys and most only go to school for a couple of years.

Schooling is free and open to everyone, so why do so few children go to school? The most important reason is that they are needed at home to work. Many families would find it very difficult to survive if their children did not work. Then, not every village has its own primary school, and secondary schools are only found in the towns and cities. Across the country, there is only one teacher to every 60 children, and one teacher cannot attend to so many children. Most parents cannot afford uniforms, books, paper and pencils for their children.

△ Feeding the chickens is one of the jobs to be done before going to school.

The Bangladesh Rural Advancement Committee (BRAC) is an organization which gives help to villages nationwide. The **World Bank** and the Canadian government are just two **donors** who have given money to BRAC. BRAC supports many activities in villages in Bangladesh. It has helped set up schools. In the schools funded by BRAC most of the pupils are girls. This is because, in the past, few women have been given the chance to learn to read and write. The BRAC schools help their pupils catch up on lessons they have missed, and try to get children back into state schools.

On Hatiya Island all the children can go to a state primary school. This opens for two to three hours every day, except Friday. (Friday is the main holy day in a mostly Muslim country like Bangladesh.) School starts early in the morning before the sun gets too hot. Children learn reading, writing and arithmetic. They also study health, farming and topics to do with village life. Classes are large, but the children are well-behaved and listen carefully to their teacher. They have reading books just like you, but most of their writing is done on tiny blackboards called **slates**, which can be used again and again.

School closes at lunch time. Children then go home to help their mothers or to work on the land. During the harvest and planting season when everyone is busy in the fields, the school closes down so that the children can help with this work.

△ A class at the primary school. The pupils can sit outside because the weather is warm.

Spare time

People who live in Bangladesh are usually very busy working on the land or in the home. Adults have little spare time to go out and there are no restaurants, swimming pools or cinemas in the countryside.

After the men's daily visit to the mosque, they will often stop and chat. There is a strong community spirit in the villages. Everybody knows everyone else and friendships are close. Meetings are held to arrange festivals and to plan for the rainy season.

Children also make their own entertainment. There is no shortage of water in Bangladesh and the weather is always warm. Children often play and swim in a nearby river or the sea. Although children are expected to work from an early age, they still find time to play. They make toys out of rushes and bamboo.

▽ Women hold a village meeting on Hatiya Island.

ople enjoy
tening to music
Bangladesh. There is
ngali music, and other sorts of music from around the
orld. There is music on the radio, and live music in
llages and towns. People enjoy dancing and watching
ays which are put on in the villages. The photograph
ove shows a play on Hatiya Island. Children are
lowed to stay up late to watch.

Bangladesh, both rich and poor people enjoy
stivals. Weddings are usually colourful events and a
ast is prepared to celebrate the occasion. Everyone in
e village is invited. People buy new clothes if they can
ford to, and dress up. They also eat special foods.

ople who have moved away from their home village
turn for festivals and family celebrations. They visit
eir family and old friends. The **Eid ul Fitr** is an
portant festival for Muslims. Hindus celebrate
urga Puja.

△ Men from
the village put on
a play for
everyone's
entertainment.

Sabjada's day

Sabjada Khatun is one of the 300,000 people who live on Hatiya Island. What is a day like for her?

Sabjada has one son and three daughters. Her husband was killed by a cyclone some years ago. She lives in Batenkhali, in the north of Hatiya. She has had to move house five times because of erosion from the rivers.

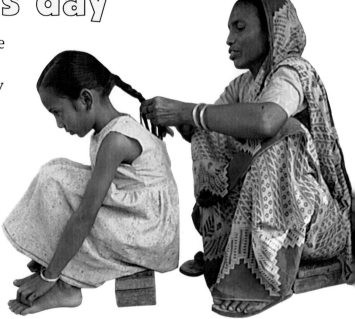

Sabjada helps one of her daughters get ready for school

Sabjada gets up at dawn. She wakes her family, rolls up the sleeping mats and sweeps out the room. She buys food for breakfast, muri (puffed rice) and milk. She makes a fire with rice straw to warm the milk. Her children get ready for school while Sabjada talks to Manja Khatun, her aunt, who lives next door.

When her children leave Sabjada goes to work. She is one of the organizers of a women's group in Batenkhali. First she goes to a meeting to talk about problems in the community.

Then Sabjada sets out on her rounds. She is a midwife, and visits women who are going to have babies. There are many children born in Batenkhali, and she is busy. At noon she stops at the fish pond to get fish for the meal that evening. Then she continues her rounds, visiting patients.

Because it gets dark early, and there is no electricity, cooking has to be done before sunset. Sabjada and her aunt, Manja Khatun, prepare the meal. Manja's grandchildren help. The meal is rice, lentils, vegetables and fish. Manja's granddaughter joins Sabjada's family for the meal. She decides to spend the night with her cousins. They sleep on mats on the floor.

In most families on Hatiya Island the women and girls collect water from the village well, prepare food, keep an eye on any animals, and look after the house. The men and older boys spend most of the day tending their crops of rice or jute. They build **embankments** to protect villages from flooding. Men usually do the family shopping.

The first time most families on Hatiya Island relax together is with the evening meal. Family members sit on the **verandah** floor to eat. After the meal there is sometimes a meeting or entertainment in the village, but usually everyone is asleep early.

The next day each family starts its day at dawn...

△ Sabjada and her family relaxing together, eating their evening meal.

▷ Tonight it is so warm that the family do not need any blankets.

Travel in Hatiya Island

These boys a used to walking man kilometres along tracks like this.

The roads are poor on Hatiya Island. There is one main road which links the north of the island to the south coast. Most of this road is little more than a raised track made of solid earth. All the villages are linked to this main road by narrow lanes. These are just wide enough for a bus to get down. During the wet season it is impossible to use the roads as they are knee-deep in soft mud.

This bus is so full that some passengers have to sit on the roof.

here is a bus stop in every village and Sabjada's village Batenkhali is no exception. No one in the village wns a car but a taxi can be called from the village store emergencies. Buses stop at the village twice a day. ney are crowded and very slow. The buses are used to ansport everything, including people and goods for arket, such as chickens and vegetables.

atenkhali is on the north coast and a few people in the llage have wooden fishing boats. It is often easier and uicker to row around the coast to another village than catch the bus. The ferry port is close to the village. The rry goes to the mainland once every day and the urney takes about two hours.

ne photograph opposite shows a track just outside a llage on Hatiya Island. The two boys are walking back the village. A mule may be used to carry a load, herwise people are used to walking many kilometres ery day. People walk to the pump for fresh water, eople walk to the paddy fields to work and children alk to school. Some families have managed to save nough money to buy a bicycle. Bicycles are an nportant form of transport in Bangladesh.

Journeys

Bangladesh is divided up by lots of rivers. It is not surprising that boats are the most important form of transport. You could travel by ferry along nearly 9000 kilometres of river. Trains have only 5000 kilometres of track. More than half of all goods and cargo are carried by boats travelling along the country's rivers.

You would have to cross many rivers to travel from east Bangladesh to the west of the country, a distance of about 400 kilometres at the widest point. There are not many road bridges because they are expensive to build. Ferries called 'steamers' are used to cross many rivers instead, but they are quite slow. It can take up to three days to travel by bus and ferry across the country, from one border to the other.

In Bangladesh roads and railways mainly follow the routes taken by rivers. For more roads and railways to be built, many new bridges would be needed. There are plans for a bridge across the River Nihamputra to link east and west Bangladesh. It will be very expensive to build and will have to be 12 kilometres long.

There are few cars in the country and so most people travel by bus, train or ferry. Journeys are slow as many of the roads are muddy, especially during the wet season. This journey was described by an Oxfam worker travelling to Hatiya Island from Dhaka:

'The trip to the island was very long, and very muddy. Eight hours by road, the last 30 kilometres at a snail's pace because the road is in a state, as the recent rain churned it up. This was followed by a boat trip of a further two hours.'

For many people living on Hatiya Island the journey has been in the opposite direction. People have moved from the island to Dhaka.

▷ Travelling in Bangladesh often crowde because the are not enou trains.

▽ Boats ferry people across th river in the city o Dhaka.

City life

As in most Asian countries, towns and cities in Bangladesh have grown quickly during the last 30 years. Thousands of Bangladeshis have migrated from the countryside to live in cities like Dhaka, Chittagong and Khulna. People have also moved to other countries in search of a better life. Some Bangladeshis work in the Gulf states. Others have **emigrated** to Canada and the USA, where they are known as East Indians. Some came to the UK, where most so-called 'Indian' restaurants are actually owned by Bangladeshis, many from the Sylhet region.

Why are people moving from the countryside to cities, or even abroad? First, people may not be able to survive in the countryside. Perhaps they do not own land and so cannot grow the food needed by their family. Their home may have been destroyed in a recent flood. Second, people may be attracted to a city because they believe there will be plenty of well-paid jobs, housing with electricity and running water, and schools and hospitals.

▽ This bustee, or slum area, has been built alongside a railway track in Dhaka.

Many people hope to find wealth in cities like Dhaka.

though life in the city is generally better than life in the country, some things are worse. Large slum areas called **bustees** have grown up around towns and cities. Homes are built from scraps of wood, tin and bamboo. In many cases they are worse than the houses which migrants left behind. People live in very crowded conditions, possibly sharing one tap and one toilet among hundreds of people.

Some people get jobs driving rickshaws. These are bicycle taxis with a human engine. There are some rickshaws in this photo of a Dhaka street. You can see rickshaws all over the country. The land is flat, so it is not too difficult to pull a rickshaw – but it is still very hard work.

Bangladeshi people have to face many problems. The main task for the next century will be to improve the lives of everyone. To do this the problem of land ownership must be tackled. If people owned land themselves, they might not feel the need to migrate to the city. After all, Bangladesh has some of the richest farmland in the world. It should be possible for everyone to take advantage of it, and to have a good standard of living.

Glossary

Bangla This is the language spoken by around 80% of the population of Bangladesh.

Biodegradable This is a term used to describe waste which contains few harmful chemicals. It decomposes without poisoning the soil or water into which it is dumped. An apple core is biodegradable as it decomposes naturally leaving no trace behind.

Contamination Water infected with germs and bacteria is contaminated. Drinking contaminated water can cause serious illness.

Cyclone A cyclone is a weather system where winds are very strong and the weather is stormy and wet.

Delta This is land which is formed at a river mouth. As a large river approaches the sea, some of the material which it has been carrying is dumped on the valley floor. This silt is rich and fertile.

Development Agency This is an organization which helps to provide jobs, housing and education. Development agencies may be funded by foreign governments or by charities such as Oxfam.

Donor To donate means to give. Richer countries donate money, goods and expertise to less wealthy countries. Some, like the Netherlands, are more generous than others.

Durga Puja A Hindu festival which celebrates the victory of the beautiful two headed goddess Durga over the buffalo-headed demon called Mahisha.

Embankment This is a raised river bank. Embankments are sometimes man-made to prevent a river from flooding.

Emigrate To move to, and settle in another country.

Export Goods which are sold to other countries are called exports.

Eid ul Fitr This is a Muslim festival which celebrates the end of the month long fast, called Ramadan. Adults only eat and drink when it is dark during Ramadan.

Imam This is the name given to some Muslim leaders. The Imam usually leads the prayers in the mosque.

Irrigation systems Irrigation is a method where water is provided to help crops grow during dry weather. Water is usually stored in reservoirs or wells and is channelled into fields when it is needed.

Killah land Here fields are built up so that they lie well above the level of a river. This prevents floods from destroying crops during the wet season.

Migration Migration means a large scale movement of animals, birds or people from one place to another.

Monsoon The monsoon is a seasonal wind which occurs in S.Asia. This term is usually used to describe the wet weather brought by the summer winds which travel over the Indian Ocean before they hit the land.

Paddy fields Rice fields are called paddys. They are small with raised banks around the outside, called bunds. Bunds allow water to b trapped inside the field so that rice can germinate under water.

Slate Slates are made of a grey rock which splits into thin slabs. They are usually the same size as a book. Children can write on slates using chalk. Slates can easily be wiped clean, so can be used again and again.

Veranda This is an open rooted platform, built along the side of a house. It may be use as living space.

Western World This term is used to group together the richer developed countries of Europe, North America, Japan, Australia and New Zealand. The people living in these part of the world have a rich standard of living.

World Bank The World Bank is operated by the United Nations. Its money comes from economically developed countries. Money is given or loaned to fund projects in poorer countries.

ndex

About Oxfam in Bangladesh

Oxfam works with poor people and their organizations in over 80 countries. Oxfam believes that all people have basic rights: to earn a living, and to have food, shelter, health care and education. Oxfam provides relief in emergencies, and gives long-term support to people struggling to build a better life for themselves and their families. Oxfam works in the north-west and south-west of Bangladesh, in some of the poorest regions of the country. Support is given to local organizations, either financially, or through help with training and organization. Many of Bangladesh's largest development organizations started with funding from Oxfam. Oxfam supports work in employment and landlessness, women's rights, education, environment and disaster-preparedness, health and disability, and tribal rights. The organizations supported by Oxfam are encouraged to address the needs and development of women.

The author and publishers would like to thank the following for their help in preparing this book: Pramod Unia, Heather Blackwell and Caroline Lequesne from the Oxfam Asia Desk; the staff at the Oxfam Dhaka office; the staff of the Oxfam photo library; and the Oxfam Education workers who commented on early drafts.

The Oxfam Education Catalogue lists a range of other resources on economically developing countries, including Bangladesh, and issues of development. These materials are produced by Oxfam, by other agencies, and by Development Education Centres. For a copy of the catalogue contact Oxfam, 274 Banbury Road, Oxford OX2 7DZ, phone (0865) 311311, or your national Oxfam office.

Photographic acknowledgements
The author and publishers wish to acknowledge, with thanks, the following photographic sources:

Panos Pictures/Barbara Klass pp2, 3, 25, 27a; Howard J. Davies p29; Oxfam R. Vesfeld p4; Dr Shahidul Alam pp5, 8, 12, 15, 16, 17, 18, 19, 20, 21, 22, 23; Walter Holt pp6, 7; Philip Jackson p9; Badal p10; Carol Wills p11; Oxfam pp13, 24, 27, 28

The publishers have made every effort to trace the copyright holders, but if they have inadvertently overlooked any, they will be pleased to make the necessary arrangement at the first opportunity.

Cover photograph © Oxfam/Shahidul Alam/Drik Photo Library – A young girl studying, on Hatiya Island.

Note to the reader - In this book there are some words in the text which are printed in **bold** type. This shows that the word is listed in the glossary on page 30. The glossary gives a brief explanation of words which may be new to you.

First published in Great Britain by Heinemann Library an imprint of Heinemann Publishers (Oxford) Ltd Halley Court, Jordan Hill, Oxford OX2 8EJ

OXFORD LONDON EDINBURGH MADRID ATHENS BOLOGNA PARIS MELBOURNE SYDNEY AUCKLAND SINGAPORE TOKYO IBADAN NAIROBI HARARE GABORONE PORTSMOUTH NH (USA)

© 1994 Heinemann Library

98 97 96 95 94
10 9 8 7 6 5 4 3 2 1

British Library Cataloguing in Publication Data is available from the British Library on request.

ISBN 0 431 07251 5 (Hardback)

ISBN 0 431 07257 4 (Paperback)

Designed and produced by Visual Image
Cover design by Threefold Design

Printed in China

954.92
8595